Places in My Community

DISCOVER!

Visiting the Library

By Seth Lynch

Enslow Publishing

Please visit our website, www.enslow.com.
For a free color catalog of all our high-quality books, call toll free 1-800-398-2504 or fax 1-877-980-4454.

Library of Congress Cataloging-in-Publication Data

Names: Lynch, Seth, author.
Title: Visiting the library / Seth Lynch.
Description: Buffalo, NY : Enslow Publishing, [2023] | Series: Places in my community | Includes index.
Identifiers: LCCN 2022018020 (print) | LCCN 2022018021 (ebook) | ISBN 9781978521384 (paperback) | ISBN 9781978521407 (library binding) | ISBN 9781978521414 (ebook)
Subjects: CYAC: Libraries–Juvenile literature.
Classification: LCC Z665.5 .L96 2023 (print) | LCC Z665.5 (ebook) | DDC 027–dc23/eng/20220521
LC record available at https://lccn.loc.gov/2022018020
LC ebook record available at https://lccn.loc.gov/2022018021

Published in 2023 by
Enslow Publishing
2544 Clinton Street
Buffalo, NY 14224

Designer: Andrea Davison-Bartolotta
Editor: Kristen Nelson

Photo credits: Cover Ferenc Szelepcsenyi/Shutterstock.com; cover, back cover, series art (town background) monbibi/Shutterstock.com; p. 4 GoodStudio/Shutterstock.com; p. 5 LightFieldStudios/iStockphoto.com; p. 6 Inspiring/Shutterstock.com; p. 7 Celig/Shutterstock.com; p. 8 Studio_G/Shutterstock.com; pp. 9, 13 wavebreakmedia/Shutterstock.com; p. 10 Sensvector/Shutterstock.com; p. 11 fizkes/Shutterstock.com; p. 12 ClassicVector/Shutterstock.com; p. 14 BRO.vector/Shutterstock.com; p. 15 Rawpixel.com/Shutterstock.com; p. 16 Alias Ching/Shutterstock.com; p. 17 New Africa/Shutterstock.com; p. 19 Tyler Olson/Shutterstock.com; p. 20 WinWin artlab/Shutterstock.com; p. 21 Sergey Novikov/Shutterstock.com.

Printed in the United States of America

CPSIA compliance information: Batch #CWENS23: For further information contact Enslow Publishing at 1-800-398-2504.

CONTENTS

Boldface words appear in Words to Know.

TO THE LIBRARY!

A library is a busy, important part of a community. The most familiar kinds of libraries are school libraries and public libraries. Public libraries are libraries where anyone in the community can go. There are **materials** for all ages!

Check when the public library is open before visiting.

GET YOUR CARD

Those who visit the library are often there to **borrow** books. They use their library card to do so. A library card tells who you are and where you live. Library cards also allow you to borrow movies, games, and magazines too!

Ask a librarian to help you sign up for a library card if you don't have one.

WHAT'S IN A LIBRARY?

Libraries do have a lot of books. Some are just for reading for fun. Others help you to learn. Many people visit the library to use the public computers. They may need to use the library's **internet access**.

You might take out a **nonfiction** book to help with a school project.

Libraries commonly have story hours, crafts, or other things for kids to do. Some have play areas and toys. Many kinds of people meet at libraries. Book clubs, knitting groups, and school **tutors** are often found there.

Book clubs are groups that all read the same book and then talk about it.

LIBRARIANS

If you visit the library, you'll see librarians! These community helpers have many jobs. Some librarians choose and buy books and movies to add to the library's **collection**. They may spend time at the library's desk to check library materials in and out.

Children's librarians are those that work with library materials for kids and kid visitors!

Other librarians help community members use the public computers. They may work with older people to learn about new **technology**. They aid those doing **research** online. Librarians also set up talks the community will learn from and enjoy.

People use library computers to stay in touch with family, find out the news, and more.

THE LIBRARY, ONLINE

Libraries have a lot going on! But you can visit the library without stepping foot in the public library building. Most libraries now have online collections. You can use your library card to take out e-books, audiobooks, or music!

Audiobooks are books that have been read out loud and recorded for someone to listen to.

TAKE IT BACK

All library materials must be returned, whether in person or online. Online materials are **automatically** returned. Books and movies you've borrowed in person have to be taken back on time. If not, you may have to pay a little money. This is called a fine.

Once you return your books, you can go look for more to check out!

A COMMUNITY SPACE

Libraries are welcoming places. They're meeting places for people of all ages and interests. They're a quiet place for doing homework or discovering a great new book or movie. Librarians help others learn. What a wonderful part of the community!

All you need to visit the library is a library card and an open mind!

WORDS TO KNOW

automatically: Happening without the control of a person.

borrow: To take and use for an amount of time before returning it.

collection: A group of things owned by a place such as a library.

internet access: The ability to use the internet, or the system that connects computers around the world.

materials: The things in a library's collection, such as books, games, movies, and magazines.

nonfiction: Writing based on facts and not made up.

research: Studying to find something new.

technology: Something created by using science, engineering, and other industries to invent useful tools or solve problems.

tutor: A person who helps a student with schoolwork.

FOR MORE INFORMATION

BOOKS

Bassier, Emma. *Libraries.* Minneapolis, MN: Cody Koala, an imprint of Pop!: 2020.

Kawa, Katie. *A Day with a Librarian.* New York, NY: Cavendish Square Publishing, 2021.

WEBSITES

ALA for Kids: Education and Careers

www.ala.org/educationcareers/libcareers/kids

Do you want to be a librarian? Visit the American Library Association's website for kids about this fun career.

TIME: The 100 Best Children's Books of All Time

time.com/100-best-childrens-books/

Check out this list to find your next library book!

Publisher's note to educators and parents: Our editors have carefully reviewed these websites to ensure that they are suitable for students. Many websites change frequently, however, and we cannot guarantee that a site's future contents will continue to meet our high standards of quality and educational value. Be advised that students should be closely supervised whenever they access the internet.

INDEX